Superstars of Wrestling

KOFI KINGSTON

BY BENJAMIN PROUDFIT

HOT TOPICS

Gareth Stevens
PUBLISHING

Please visit our website, www.garethstevens.com. For a free color catalog of all our high-quality books, call toll free 1-800-542-2595 or fax 1-877-542-2596.

Library of Congress Cataloging-in-Publication Data

Names: Proudfit, Benjamin, author.
Title: Kofi Kingston / Benjamin Proudfit.
Description: New York : Gareth Stevens Publishing, 2022. | Series: Superstars of wrestling | Includes index.
Identifiers: LCCN 2020032251 (print) | LCCN 2020032252 (ebook) | ISBN 9781538265956 (library binding) | ISBN 9781538265932 (paperback) | ISBN 9781538265949 (set) | ISBN 9781538265963 (ebook)
Subjects: LCSH: Kingston, Kofi, 1981---Juvenile literature. | World Wrestling Entertainment, Inc.--Biography--Juvenile literature. | Wrestlers--Ghana--Biography--Juvenile literature.
Classification: LCC GV1196.K62 P76 2022 (print) | LCC GV1196.K62 (ebook) | DDC 796.812092 [B]--dc23
LC record available at https://lccn.loc.gov/2020032251
LC ebook record available at https://lccn.loc.gov/2020032252

First Edition

Published in 2022 by
Gareth Stevens Publishing
29 E. 21st Street
New York, NY 10010

Copyright © 2022 Gareth Stevens Publishing

Designer: Michael Flynn
Editor: Kristen Nelson

Photo credits: Cover, pp. 1, 25 Amer Hilabi/AFP/Getty Images; pp. 5, 9, 11 Icon Sport/Getty Images; p. 7 Jason Merritt/Getty Images; p. 13 Moses Robinson/Getty Images; p. 15 Chris Weeks/WWE/Getty Images; p. 17 JP Yim/Stringer/Getty Images; p. 19 Marc Pfitzenreuter/Getty Images; p. 21 Adam Pretty/Bongarts/Getty Images; p. 23 Chris Ryan/Corbis Sport/Getty Images; p. 27 Ethan Miller/Getty Images; p. 29 Bauzen/GC Images/Getty Images.

All rights reserved. No part of this book may be reproduced in any form without permission in writing from the publisher, except by a reviewer.

Printed in the United States of America

CPSIA compliance information: Batch #CSGS22: For further information contact Gareth Stevens, New York, New York at 1-800-542-2595.

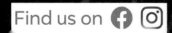

CONTENTS

Amazing Kofi	4
From the Start	6
Going Pro	10
Champ!	12
Part of the Team	14
The New Day Dawns	16
Road to WrestleMania	22
Back to Tagging	26
Next for Kofi	28
The Best of Kofi Kingston	30
For More Information	31
Glossary	32
Index	32

AMAZING KOFI

Kofi Kingston is one of the most accomplished superstars in World Wrestling Entertainment (WWE) today. He's a member of one of the most successful wrestling **stables** in WWE. And he's one of only four Black men to ever hold the WWE Championship.

IN THE RING

Kofi is known for his high-flying moves, especially during his many Royal Rumble appearances!

5

FROM THE START

Kofi Sarkodie-Mensah was born in Ghana, West Africa, on August 14, 1981. He moved to the United States when he was 2 years old. He was the captain of the **amateur** wrestling team at his Massachusetts high school.

IN THE RING

Kofi went to Boston College. He graduated, or finished school, in 2003.

7

Kofi dreamed of being a top **professional** wrestler, but he was always told he was too small. After college, he worked in advertising. He said later: "I stopped following my dreams … but in my heart, I wanted to be in the WWE."

IN THE RING

Kofi is billed as, or said to be, 6 feet (1.8 m) tall and 212 pounds (96 kg).

GOING PRO

In 2006, Kofi signed a **developmental** deal with WWE. He started wrestling under the name Kofi Kingston. Kofi made his **debut** on the WWE *ECW* TV show in January 2008. By June, he was on *Raw* and won his first Intercontinental Championship!

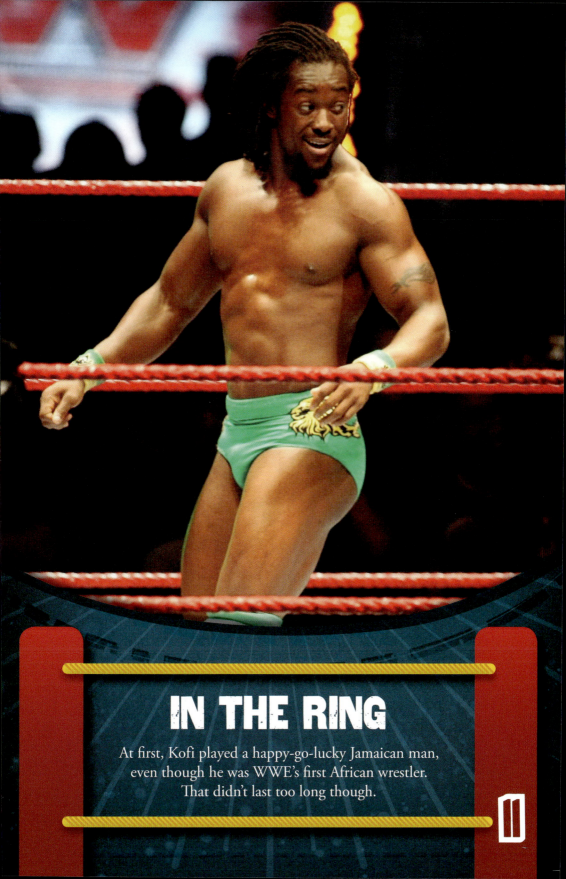

IN THE RING

At first, Kofi played a happy-go-lucky Jamaican man, even though he was WWE's first African wrestler. That didn't last too long though.

CHAMP!

Kofi went on to win the Intercontinental title three more times. He also was United States Champion twice. In 2009, he beat a wrestler named MVP for the U.S. title. Kofi also took on Sheamus and won the U.S. belt at Extreme Rules in 2011.

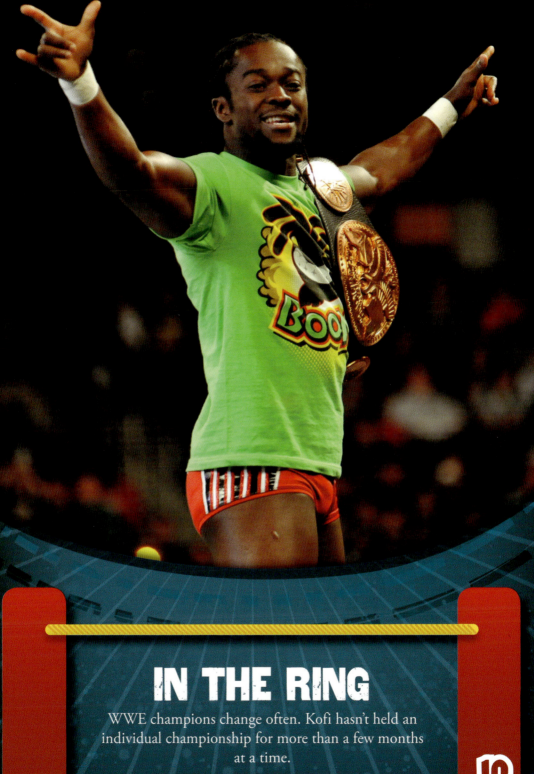

IN THE RING

WWE champions change often. Kofi hasn't held an individual championship for more than a few months at a time.

PART OF THE TEAM

Between individual championship wins, Kofi lit up the tag team **division**. His first World Tag Team title came with CM Punk in 2008. He and Evan Bourne won the WWE Tag Team title in 2011. Kofi won that title again with R-Truth in 2012.

R-TRUTH

IN THE RING

In 2011, Kofi was on the winning team in an eight-man tag team **match** at WrestleMania 27. He took part in a tag match in 2012 at WrestleMania 28 too.

THE NEW DAY DAWNS

By 2013, Kofi wasn't being used on TV much. He was ready for something new. He teamed up with Big E and Xavier Woods in 2014 to form the tag team The New Day. They debuted in November 2014.

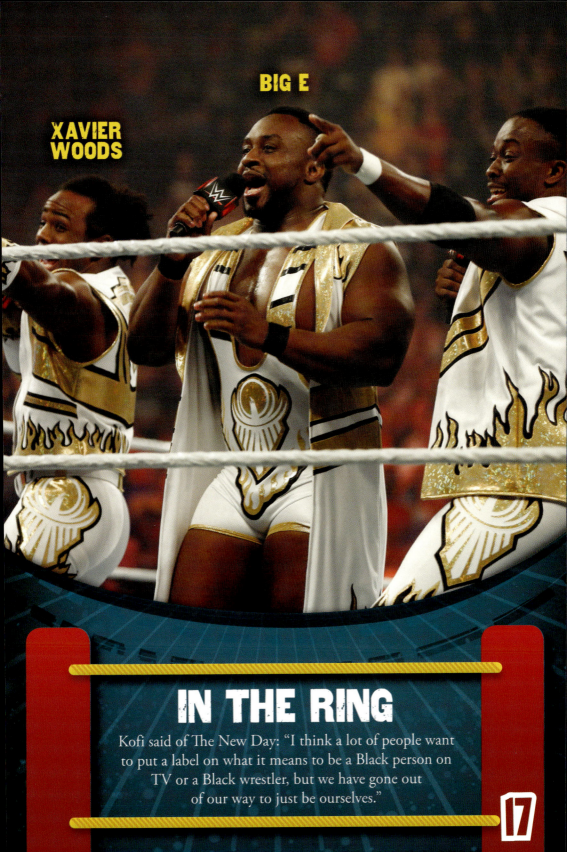

IN THE RING

Kofi said of The New Day: "I think a lot of people want to put a label on what it means to be a Black person on TV or a Black wrestler, but we have gone out of our way to just be ourselves."

At first, The New Day were booed by fans. But their in-ring work and fun ideas won over the WWE universe. The New Day won their first WWE Tag Team Championship at Extreme Rules in April 2015.

IN THE RING

At times, The New Day have been the top sellers of WWE merchandise, or items like T-shirts, hats, and action figures.

The New Day would go on to win another WWE Tag Team Championship, as well as many SmackDown Tag Team Championships. They became the longest-reigning tag team champions in WWE history! They hosted WrestleMania 33 in 2017.

IN THE RING

The New Day have performed as both good guys, or babyfaces, and bad guys, or heels.

ROAD TO WRESTLEMANIA

Kingston didn't take part in many singles matches once The New Day started. But in 2019, he was put into the spotlight, earning his way into a match at WrestleMania 35. He would face the heel, Daniel Bryan, for the WWE Championship.

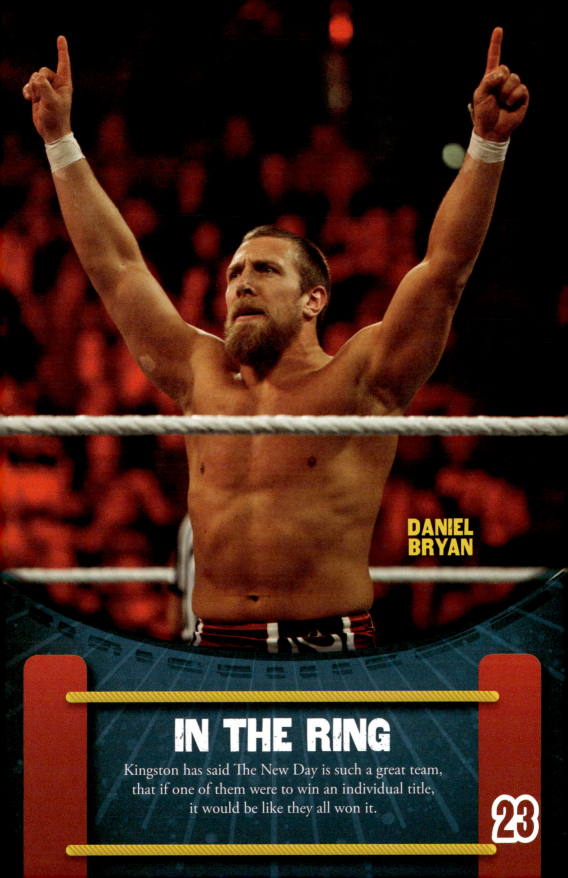

DANIEL BRYAN

IN THE RING

Kingston has said The New Day is such a great team, that if one of them were to win an individual title, it would be like they all won it.

Kofi started the match against Daniel Bryan as the fan favorite. He faced kicks, running knees, and Bryan's LeBell Lock. It was Kofi's finisher, trouble in paradise, that would win him the title. His sons joined him in the ring after his win!

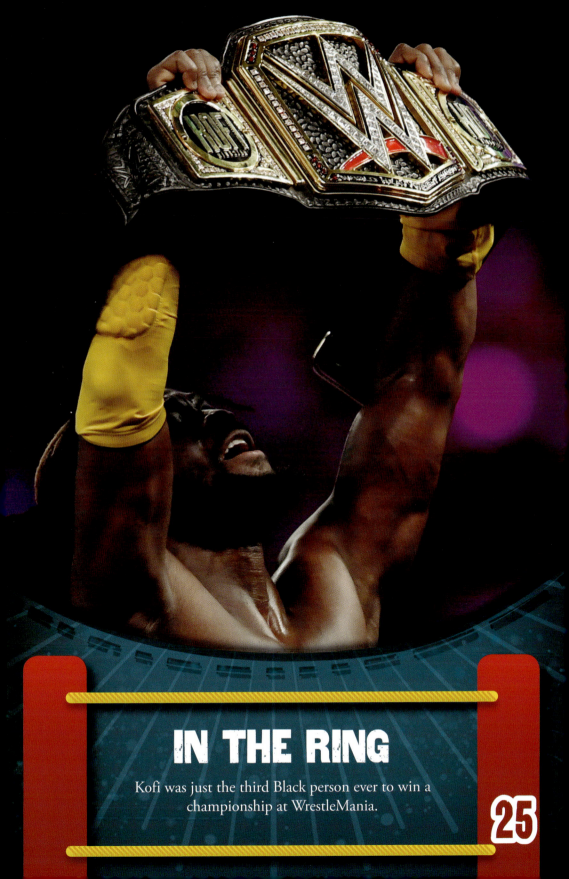

IN THE RING

Kofi was just the third Black person ever to win a championship at WrestleMania.

25

BACK TO TAGGING

Kofi held the title until October 2019. He faced Brock Lesnar, but was met with Brock's F-5, and lost the title. Kofi returned to wrestling with The New Day. They went on to win the SmackDown Tag Team Championship again!

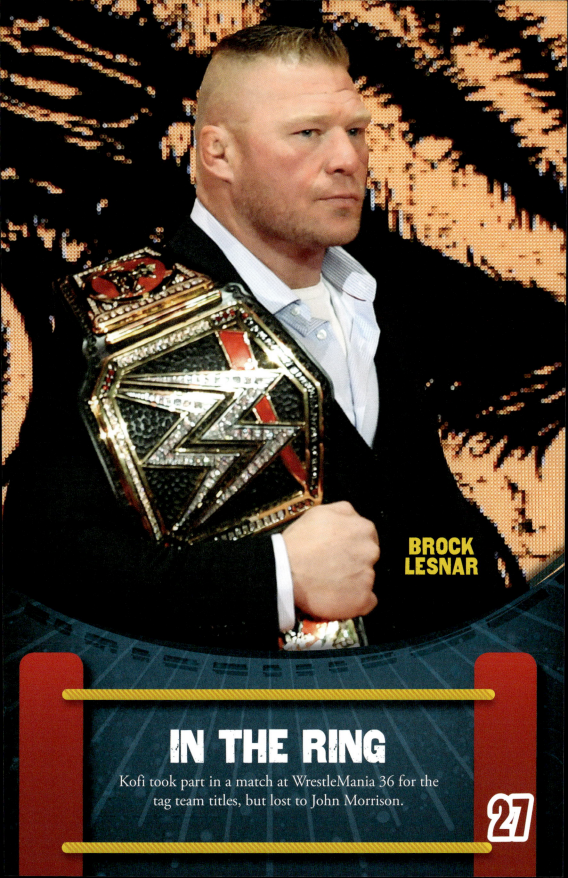

BROCK LESNAR

IN THE RING

Kofi took part in a match at WrestleMania 36 for the tag team titles, but lost to John Morrison.

27

NEXT FOR KOFI

Kofi Kingston has been a big part of the WWE for more than 15 years. His success on his own and with The New Day shows how good he is in the ring and how much fans love him. What's next for Kofi?

IN THE RING

In 2020, Kofi starred in the Netflix movie *The Main Event* alongside the Miz and Sheamus.

THE BEST OF KOFI KINGSTON

SIGNATURE MOVES
boom drop, hurricanrana

FINISHERS
S.O.S., trouble in paradise

ACCOMPLISHMENTS
WWE Intercontinental Champion
WWE United States Champion
WWE Tag Team Champion
SmackDown Tag Team Champion
WWE Champion

MATCHES TO WATCH
WrestleMania 35 vs. Daniel Bryan; The New Day vs. The Shield at Survivor Series 2017

FOR MORE INFORMATION

BOOKS

Borth, Teddy. *The New Day: The Power of Positivity*. Minneapolis, MN: Abdo Zoom, 2018.

Miller, Dean. *Beyond Extreme*. New York, NY: DK Publishing, 2020.

WEBSITES

Kofi Kingston—WWE
www.wwe.com/superstars/kofi-kingston
Keep up to date on Kofi's career with his official superstar profile.

WWE News, Video—ESPN
www.espn.com/wwe/
Check out ESPN's coverage of the WWE here!

Publisher's note to educators and parents: Our editors have carefully reviewed these websites to ensure that they are suitable for students. Many websites change frequently, however, and we cannot guarantee that a site's future contents will continue to meet our high standards of quality and educational value. Be advised that students should be closely supervised whenever they access the internet.

GLOSSARY

amateur: having to do with the kind of wrestling done on school teams and in the Olympics

debut: a first appearance

developmental: having to do with the growth of something or someone

division: a group of teams or people that compete against each other

match: a contest between two or more people

professional: earning money from an activity that many people do for fun

stable: in pro wrestling, a group that often performs and competes together

INDEX

Big E 16, 17
Boston College 7
Bourne, Evan 14
Bryan, Daniel 22, 23, 24
ECW 10
Ghana, West Africa 6
high school 6
Lesnar, Brock 26, 27
Main Event, The 29
MVP 12
New Day, The 16, 17, 18, 20, 22, 23, 26, 28
Raw 10
Royal Rumble 5
R-Truth 14, 15
Sheamus 12, 29
tag teams 14, 15, 16, 18, 20, 26, 27
Woods, Xavier 16, 17
WrestleMania 15, 20, 22, 24, 25, 27